Elvis Presley
The King of Rock 'n' Roll

Liz Gogerly

HODDER
Wayland

an imprint of Hodder Children's Books

© 2003 White-Thomson Publishing Ltd

Produced by White-Thomson Publishing Ltd
2/3 St Andrew's Place, Lewes, BN7 1UP

Editor: Elaine Fuoco-Lang
Inside and cover design: Tim Mayer
Picture Research: Shelley Noronha –
    Glass Onion Pictures
Proofreader: Jane Colgan

Cover: Elvis at the start of his career.
Title page: Elvis performing on stage in the 1950s.

Published in Great Britain in 2003 by Hodder Wayland,
an imprint of Hodder Children's Books

The right of Liz Gogerly to be identified as the author of
this Work has been asserted by her in accordance with the
Copyright, Designs and Patents Act 1988

British Library Cataloguing in Publication Data
Gogerly, Liz
    Elvis Presley. - (Famous lives)
    1.Presley, Elvis, 1935-1977 - Juvenile literature 2.Rock
    musicians - United States - Biography - Juvenile
    literature
    3.Motion picture actors and actresses - United States -
    Biography - Juvenile literature
    I.Title
    782.4'2'166'092

ISBN 0 7502 4322 8

Printed in Hong Kong

Hodder Children's Books
An imprint of Hodder Headline Limited
338 Euston Road, London, NW1 3BH

Picture acknowledgements
Corbis 4, 12, 13, 19, 21, 32; Pictorial Press cover, title
page, 5, 6, 10, 11, 14, 20, 22, 29, 37, 42; Popperfoto 25,
26, 27, 28, 31, 33, 36, 38, 39, 41; Redferns 7, 8, 9, 15,
17, 18, 23, 24, 30, 35, 40; Topham 16, 34, 43, 44, 45.

Jul,614   £13-81

Contents

The King of Rock 'n' Roll

People tuning in to the *Milton Berle Show* can hardly believe their eyes. It is 5 June 1956 and Elvis Presley is making one of his first television appearances. The 21-year-old ex-truck driver from Tennessee looks untamed and dangerous as he sings a rock 'n' roll number called *Hound Dog*. From the tips of his clicking fingers to his shuffling shoes his body moves to the beat of the music. When his hips gyrate, the crowd screams for more.

*Elvis performing live in Memphis in July 1956. A few weeks later **Hound Dog** was at number one on the American billboard charts.*

Gold disks decorate the walls of Elvis's home, Graceland. Elvis earned gold, platinum and multi-platinum awards for 131 albums and singles in America alone.

'The bad taste that is exemplified by the Elvis Presley 'Hound Dog' music, with his animal gyrations which are certainly most distasteful to me, are violative of all that I know to be in good taste.' Congressman Emanuel Celler in *Almost Grown: The Rise of Rock.*

In the early 1950s the popular charts were dominated by singers aimed at an older audience. The arrival of Elvis Presley was like an explosion: at last teenagers had somebody with whom they could identify. Many parents were horrified at Elvis's 'obscene' behaviour on stage, yet within a year of his appearance on the *Milton Berle Show* he was the top-selling performer of all time. In his lifetime it is estimated that Elvis sold over one billion records worldwide – more than any other recording artist – but he's most remembered for introducing the world to rock 'n' roll music. Although he died back in 1977, Elvis Presley is still revered as the King of Rock 'n' Roll.

Growing up in Mississippi

Elvis Aaron Presley was born on 8 January 1935 in the town of Tupelo, Mississippi. Elvis's twin brother – Jess Garon – died at birth so Vernon and Gladys Presley cherished their surviving child. The 1930s were known as The Great Depression and life in Tupelo was tough. Vernon drifted from one odd-job to the next trying to support his family. Then, in 1938, he was jailed for forging a cheque.

Elvis, aged about three, with his parents Vernon and Gladys.

Times were hard when Elvis was a young boy as his parents didn't have much money. To amuse himself, Elvis would make cars out of apple crates to play with, or go fishing.

'Don't you worry none, Baby. When I grow up, I'm going to buy you a fine house and pay everything you owe at the grocery store and get two Cadillacs – one for you and Daddy, and one for me.'
Gladys Presley remembering what Elvis told her when he was a young boy in *Last Train to Memphis*.

Vernon was released from prison after eight months but during this time Gladys couldn't keep up the repayments on the loan for their house and she and Elvis had lived with relatives. Throughout Elvis's childhood, the Presleys moved from one rented place to the next as Vernon tried to make a living. As an adult Elvis rarely spoke about his childhood other than to say it had been hard. Amongst his best memories were the times he listened to the *Grand Ole Opry*, a live radio show from Nashville, Tennessee that played country, gospel, bluegrass and hillbilly music every Saturday night.

First Guitar

At his first school the teacher described Elvis as 'sweet and average'. However, it was outside school hours that Elvis showed a flair for music. Elvis longed to sing love songs like the local performer Mississippi Slim and in 1944 he actually got to sing with his hero on stage. When he was ten he sang in his first talent competition and came fifth. His parents bought him a guitar for his eleventh birthday and he taught himself how to play. On Saturdays he usually went to Tupelo's jamboree to watch the hillbilly entertainers.

The Presleys were religious and regularly attended church. From an early age Elvis sang with his parents in church choirs.

When Elvis moved to Milam Junior High in 1946 he was considered a lonely misfit. Soon afterwards, the Presleys moved to a respectable coloured neighbourhood of Tupelo. It was an area where many blacks lived, at a time when blacks and whites usually lived in different neighbourhoods. Now Elvis was listening to the gospel music that poured out of the local black churches. He also began taking his guitar to school every day but was teased about his playing. Some classmates called his music 'white-trash' hillbilly or 'race' music, and one time a gang of boys cut the strings of his guitar.

Elvis's birthplace and childhood home in Tupelo.

The Shy Boy

The blues singer B.B. King at a Memphis radio station in 1950. Elvis often heard him playing live or deejaying on the radio.

In 1948 the Presleys moved to Memphis, Tennessee. Money was so tight that sometimes they ate only corn bread and water. Elvis enrolled at Humes High School but his close relationship with his mother and his inability to make new friends meant he was teased for being a 'mama's boy'. Gladys was determined that her son would graduate from High School and in his first year he got an A in language and Bs in history and physical education. Elvis was disappointed that he was given a C for music.

> 'We had to put the lights out before he'd sing ... We had a fire in the fireplace, but it wasn't enough light to show his face. He got way over yonder in the corner – that's just how shy he was.'
> Elvis's Aunt Lillian describing the times when Elvis sang in her living room, in *Last Train to Memphis*.

The city of Memphis was famous for its music, and in the 1940s black blues singers like Howlin' Wolf and B.B. King were making a name there. By the early 1950s, the blues and black gospel songs were influencing white music but at this time there were separate black and white radio stations and record companies. Many whites didn't want their children to be influenced by black music. When Elvis tuned into the local Memphis radio stations he was inspired by all the music he heard, including black music. At night he sat outside his home, quietly strumming his guitar.

Elvis, aged about 15, with his first girlfriend Betty McMann. Even as a shy teenager Elvis loved to be around women.

The Lights of Main Street

While he was still in high school, Elvis took odd jobs working in factories or theatres. The extra money meant he could indulge his new love of extravagant clothes. At school, Elvis really stood out in his unusual clothes. His hair was different too, as he greased it back with rose oil and vaseline and grew sideburns. He made a few friends but he was teased about his new look, and banned from the football team because he refused to cut off his quiff.

An early publicity photograph of Elvis. He didn't dye his light brown hair black until late 1956.

Beale Street, Memphis as it looks today. In the 1950s it was bustling with Cadillacs, and filled with music venues and shops.

'Here was this classroom full of guys in jeans and T-shirts ... and in the middle sat a dark-haired, dark-eyed boy in a pink sports coat, pink and black pants with regimental stripes down each side.'
George Klein, one of Elvis's school friends from senior year, describing the first time he noticed Elvis, in *Down at the End of Lonely Street: The Life and Death of Elvis Presley.*

Elvis's fascination with music was fuelled by his trips to the shops and theatres on Main Street and Beale Street in downtown Memphis. He began hanging out at record shops like 'Charlies' and listening to the jukebox. At the all-night gospel singings he'd marvel at the beauty and power of spiritual music. He listened carefully and tried to copy the style at home. At the school talent show in April 1953 he finally made an impression on his classmates. They were moved by the quiet intensity of his voice. Nobody was more surprised than Elvis at how popular he became after that.

The Big Break

In June 1953 Elvis graduated from high school and took a job in a factory. That summer he made a recording of two ballads for his mother's birthday at Sam Phillips' Memphis Recording Service.

When Phillips heard Elvis sing for the first time, he described his voice as 'interesting'. It was a year later when Phillips needed a vocalist for a new ballad that he remembered the shy teenager with the promising voice.

Though Elvis never wrote any of the songs he sang, he could play the guitar and piano and enjoyed jamming.

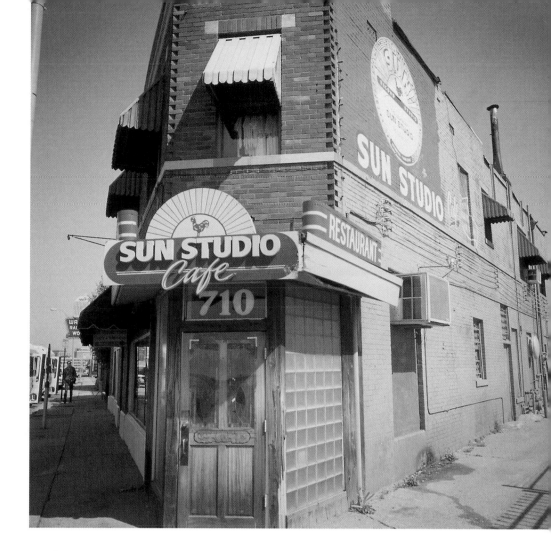

Sun Studio in Memphis is often referred to as the birthplace of rock 'n' roll. As well as Elvis, stars like Jerry Lee Lewis and Carl Perkins also recorded here.

Elvis was 19, working as a truck driver, and ready to settle down with his girlfriend Dixie Locke. However, at this next session, Phillips recognized there was something special about Elvis, and in July 1954 Elvis recorded *That's Alright Mama*. Phillips got so excited by Elvis's raw vocals and the foot-tapping beat that he asked a local DJ called Dewey Phillips to play the record on his show. It had the vitality of black music but it was sung by a white man. Nobody had heard anything like it before. When the song finished playing, the switchboard was jammed with people requesting that he play it again. Within the month, Elvis signed to Sun Records and *That's Alright Mama* was a regional hit.

'Over and over I remember Sam saying, "If I could find a white man who had the Negro sound and the Negro feel, I could make a billion dollars". This is what I heard in Elvis.'
Sam Phillips's secretary Marion Keisker describing the first time she heard Elvis sing, in *Almost Grown: The Rise of Rock*.

Overnight Sensation

On 10 August 1954 Elvis made his first live appearance at Memphis Overton Park. Within months, concerts in his hometown were filled with screaming fans. Newspapers raved about the new musical sensation describing his sound as a fusion of country and black rhythm and blues; a style of music that was becoming known as rock 'n' roll.

Rock 'n' roll wasn't new. The first white rock 'n' roll group to hit the American pop charts was Bill Haley and the Comets in 1953. Though teenagers loved their sound, Haley didn't have the looks or charisma to become the King of Rock 'n' Roll.

People hadn't seen anything like Elvis before. Female fans screamed hysterically and men tried to copy him.

Elvis signs autographs for his fans. By 1956 queues of people waited outside his parents' house all day to try and catch a glimpse of him.

'He was a typical teenager. Kind of wild, but ... in a mischievous kind of way. He loved his pranks and practical jokes ... His parents were very protective. His mother would corner me and say "Take care of my boy. Make sure he eats..."'
Scotty Moore, from Elvis's early band in *Last Train to Memphis*.

From October 1954 to 1955 Elvis played in towns throughout the South. He had a special relationship with his fans and always found time to sign autographs. Gladys and Vernon worried about their son's new career. His father didn't think there was a future in playing the guitar, and his mother missed him terribly while he was away from home. Elvis's girlfriend Dixie hoped that fame wouldn't change him. Nobody guessed just how big Elvis was about to become.

Storming up the Charts

One person who saw the potential in Elvis Presley was businessman Colonel Thomas Parker. The Colonel became Elvis's manager in mid-1955, and would remain so for the rest of Elvis's life. By this time Elvis had released five singles, which had all done well in the South, but the Colonel wanted national stardom. He struck a new deal with the major record label RCA who paid £22,500 for Elvis. At this time this was the highest sum ever paid for a pop star.

Elvis with Colonel Tom Parker. The Colonel never lost an opportunity to make money from his star.

In January 1956 Elvis released *Heartbreak Hotel*. With blues piano and a slow electric guitar solo it didn't have the usual fast-paced rock 'n' roll sound. RCA began to panic about their new signing but in March *Heartbreak Hotel* finally reached the charts. When he sang it live on the Dorsey brother's 'Stage Show' on television, record sales began to rocket. On 21 April, *Heartbreak Hotel* jumped to the number one spot and stayed there for eight weeks.

Elvis performing in the studio in January 1956. By April he was at number one in the charts in the USA.

'The colored folks been singing it and playing it just like I'm doing now, man, for more years than I know ... I got it from them.'
Elvis talking about his music in an interview from 1956, in *Last Train to Memphis*.

More Smash Hits

Elvis's hip gyrations and suggestive dance moves stirred his audiences into a frenzy.

In April 1956 Elvis played live in Las Vegas, the entertainment capital of the USA. Elvis was nervous about playing there but by now he was a superstar. That year he released singles including *Hound Dog*, *Blue Suede Shoes*, and *Love Me Tender*. Fans had never seen or heard anything like him before. His smile melted hearts and his songs stirred people's emotions. All his singles stormed to the top of the charts in the USA and UK, making Elvis a household name throughout the world. Wherever he went, fans mobbed him and the media trailed him. Even the FBI (Federal Bureau of Investigation) began to monitor his shows because they believed his act was too sexual. But somehow Elvis remained the same charming country boy he'd always been.

'I want the folks back home to think right of me. Just because I managed to do a little something, I don't want anyone back home to think I got a big head.'
Elvis in an interview with *Press-Scimitar* in Las Vegas, 1956, in *Last Train to Memphis*.

By the end of 1956 Elvis was feeling the pressure of fame. The support from his fans helped to keep him going.

Fame came at a price. The pressure of touring and promoting his new singles meant he couldn't spend much time with his new girlfriend, June Juanico. But his biggest problem was lack of sleep. Sometimes he could only grab a few hours sleep, and often he was plagued by terrible nightmares.

Lights, Camera, Action!

*A publicity poster for Elvis's first film **Love Me Tender**. In most of his future films, Elvis always got the girl but in this film he dies.*

When Elvis stepped in front of television cameras for the first time his fans were stunned by his brooding good looks. In March 1956 the Colonel arranged a Hollywood screen test and signed Elvis for a three-picture deal. In his first role in the film *Love Me Tender* Elvis played an unlucky-in-love cowboy who is killed in a shootout. When the film opened in November 1956 it was an immediate hit, and its theme tune went to number one in the USA.

'I've made a study of poor Jimmy Dean. I've made a study of myself, and I know why girls, at least the young 'uns, go for us. We're sullen, we're brooding, we're something of a menace.'
Elvis speaking to a reporter in 1956, in *Almost Grown: The Rise of Rock*.

In 1957 Elvis filmed *Loving You* and *Jailhouse Rock*. While Elvis bedazzled his fans with his on-screen presence, the soundtracks from the movies went to the top of the charts. It was a winning combination that propelled Elvis further into the spotlight, and further away from his rock 'n' roll roots. He spent less time playing live and touring, and more time in Hollywood making films, dating beautiful actresses and enjoying his new found wealth. During his lifetime Elvis made thirty films, of which the earliest films are widely recognized as his best.

In the film Jailhouse Rock *from 1957 Elvis played a rock star with a prison background.*

The Big Time

Elvis stands in front
of his new home,
Graceland. He thought
the old-fashioned
mansion would make
his mother happy.

When Elvis celebrated his 22nd birthday in 1957 he was
already a millionaire, earning more than any other entertainer
in the world. Elvis loved to collect cars and motorbikes,
and by the end of 1956 he had bought two Harley Davidson
bikes and three Cadillacs. In March 1957 he finally bought
a home befitting his superstar status. Graceland was an elegant
mansion situated on the outskirts of Memphis. He moved
in with his parents and began turning it into the house of
his dreams. Elvis insisted his mother had a beautiful bedroom,
and he also built her a chicken coop in the garden so she'd
feel more at home in her grand surroundings.

Elvis is a special guest at the launch of the charity 'Teens against Polio' held in New York in January 1957.

'I never expected to be anybody important. Maybe I'm not now, but whatever I am, whatever I will become will be what God has chosen for me ... I just want to let a few people know that the way I live is by doing what I think God wants me to.'
Elvis Presley in an interview with *Photoplay* magazine in 1958, *in Last Train to Memphis*.

Despite his lavish home, Elvis remained fairly unchanged in himself. He still preferred his mother's cooking, especially favourites like double-batter fried chicken and deep-fried banana-and-peanut-butter sandwiches. At this time he didn't indulge in drinking, smoking or taking drugs, though he still had a weakness for girls. Elvis never forgot his humble background either, and hosted charity shows to benefit disabled children and the Elvis Presley Youth Centre in Tupelo.

Saying Goodbyes

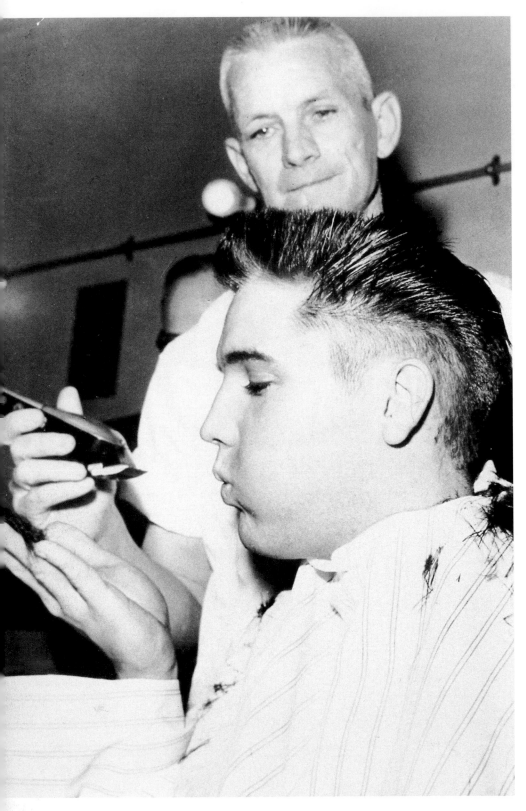

On 25 March 1958 a crowd of photographers and reporters gathered to watch Elvis's famous quiff being shaved off to be replaced with the standard GI (General Infantryman) haircut. Elvis had been called up for two years of national service and he was off to join the army. The millionaire star would now earn just £50 a month as a soldier. Thousands of fans had written letters to protest against his draft. Elvis wasn't pleased about joining the army either but he recognized it was his duty.

'Hair today, gone tomorrow,' says Elvis as his hair is cut into the traditional GI haircut.

By summer 1958 'Private Presley' was posted to Fort Hood in Texas to complete his army training. Although he lived off base with his parents, he worked hard preparing for his overseas posting in Germany. In private, he felt homesick and worried that his fans would forget him while he was away and it would be the end of his musical career. It seemed that things couldn't get any worse, but then in August, his mother died from liver disease. At her funeral Elvis nearly collapsed with grief. When he boarded the train on his way to Germany that September he looked sad and lost, like a man saying goodbye to his past.

'Mother was always right with me all my life. And it wasn't only like losing a mother, it was like losing a friend, a companion, someone to talk to ...'
Elvis talking about the loss of his mother in a press conference before he left for Germany, in *Last Train to Memphis.*

Elvis kisses his beloved mother goodbye when he joins the US Army in March 1958. Less than six months later she was dead.

A GI in Germany

Elvis wanted to be just like the other soldiers. While he was stationed in Germany he refused to make records for RCA and turned down all requests to entertain the troops. However, when he was greeted in Germany by 1,500 fans, it was obvious that life in the army would never be regular for Private Presley. Within days his request to live off base with his father and his grandmother, who had also moved to Germany, was accepted and he was given a driver to help keep him out of the public eye.

Even famous stars have to clean their own boots in the army. Elvis looks tired and sad in this photograph taken in Germany in November 1958.

Elvis had many girlfriends while he was in Germany but Priscilla was special.

'He flat-out attacked each duty, each task, as if he were storming a beachhead. This guy could soldier just as proficiently [well] as he could sing. He was the roughest, toughest … soldier I ever had under my command.'
Elvis's former commanding officer Colonel William J. Taylor Jr. describing Elvis as a soldier, in *Down at the End of Lonely Street.*

Despite his special treatment Elvis was a good soldier who was popular with the other men too. At his home in Bad Nauheim he hosted parties, and sang his favourite gospel songs for his friends. It was during one of these parties that he met Priscilla Beaulieu, the daughter of an army captain. Although she was just 14 years old, Elvis couldn't keep his eyes off her and soon they were meeting in secret because Priscilla was so young.

Around this time, Elvis had another secret too. To help him stay awake for his late-night parties and early-morning duties at base he began to take prescription tablets.

The King is Back!

In March 1960 Elvis said goodbye to Priscilla and army life and returned home to Graceland. Two years before, Elvis had sold a record-breaking 18 million singles – to date no other artist has beaten that record. That May, when his new single *Stuck on You* was a hit in the USA and UK, it seemed he still had that old magic. The next test came when he appeared on the show *Welcome Home, Elvis*, hosted by the 'King of Crooners', Frank Sinatra. Years earlier Sinatra had called Elvis's music 'deplorable'. The meeting of the two 'Kings' could have been a disaster but Elvis proved he could still compete with the best entertainers in the world.

Elvis and Sinatra sang together on the **Welcome Home, Elvis** *show. When it was shown in May 1960 nearly 68 per cent of US television viewers tuned in.*

> **'If I don't please the audience, the money don't mean nothing.'**
> Elvis in a interview with the *Nashville Tennessean*, March 1960, in *Elvis Day by Day*.

Elvis on the set of GI Blues in July 1960. In this comedy-musical Elvis plays a soldier posted to Germany.

That year Elvis had number one hits with the old-fashioned ballad *Are You Lonesome Tonight?* and the love song *It's Now or Never*. Most fans remained loyal to Elvis but some began to wonder if the army had tamed him completely – just what had happened to his wild, gutsy style of music?

When Elvis returned to Hollywood to make films like *GI Blues* and *Flaming Star* it looked like he'd turned his back on rock 'n' roll for good.

A Life like the Movies

In March 1961 Elvis played live in Honolulu, Hawaii. The crowd went crazy as Elvis delivered one of the best performances of his life. Unfortunately for his fans they wouldn't see him play live again for nearly eight years. Elvis's film career grew over this time as he starred in *Blue Hawaii* and *Viva Las Vegas* with gorgeous leading ladies in exotic locations. Sadly, the plots had become too predictable and Elvis began to resent the deals made by the Colonel that kept him tied to Hollywood.

In the comedy-musical, Blue Hawaii (1962), Elvis leaves the army and takes a job with the Hawaii tourist agency. Life is rosy until too much attention from a group of schoolgirls threatens his relationship with his girlfriend.

When Elvis finally married Priscilla in 1967 it looked like a real-life fairy tale.

> *'I ... became very interested reading about religions. I was interested in self-realization – in finding one's true self. Who isn't? [But] I have never left my own church.'*
> Elvis explaining his search for spirituality to May Mann, a Hollywood gossip columnist, in *Careless Love: The Unmaking of Elvis Presley*.

As he became older, he became more spiritual as he searched for answers about his own life, but in other ways he became wilder. He surrounded himself with a gang of friends, who became known as 'the Memphis Mafia', to act as his constant bodyguards. They hosted all-night parties and Elvis dated a string of beautiful women. Meanwhile Priscilla Beaulieu had secretly moved into Graceland where she waited patiently for Elvis to marry her. They were eventually married in 1967 and nine months later they had a daughter who they named Lisa Marie.

A New Era

In 1964 a new band from England called the Beatles was creating the kind of sensation that Elvis had been in 1956. The Beatles had been inspired by Elvis, but when they met their hero in August 1965 they were disappointed. Conversation didn't flow and John Lennon asked Elvis when he'd get back to playing proper rock 'n' roll. This historic meeting did however make Elvis more determined to play live, and record music with more meaning and soul.

In 1964 the Beatles had their first number one in the USA. Unlike Elvis, John Lennon and Paul McCartney wrote their own songs.

'I will never sing a song I don't believe in again. I will never make another movie I don't believe in again.'
Elvis in 1968 following the success of his television special, in *Down at the End of Lonely Street*.

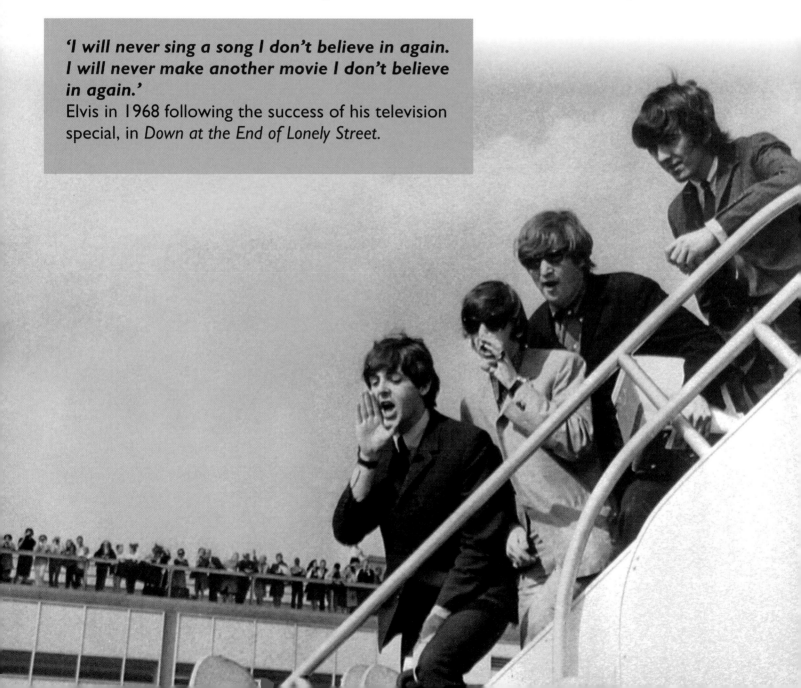

When he appeared on the 1968 special, wearing black leather, Elvis looked sleek and sounded raw and untamed again.

It was not until 1968 that Elvis finally performed live again. At the end of the show he sang *If I Can Dream*. It was the first time that Elvis had sung a song that addressed the current situation in his country. It was the year black leader Martin Luther King and presidential candidate Robert Kennedy had been assassinated, and American troops were fighting in Vietnam. The following year he released *In the Ghetto*, a moving song about poverty in the black ghettos of northern American cities. Later that year, when the soulful *Suspicious Minds* went to number one, it seemed like Elvis had found his former magic.

Behind the Dazzling Smile

Many people believed that Elvis's comeback was partly due to the happiness he'd found as a family man. They thought his marriage to Priscilla was like a fairy tale, but in truth Elvis neglected his new wife. He preferred the company of the Memphis Mafia, and he never stopped dating other women. Elvis had also become more dependent on prescription drugs. These brought on mood swings and panic attacks.

'During the lulls he wouldn't know what to do with himself. He was like a child. He would take pills or read or just eat — because he was bored. You know, he just had to occupy his time with something to do.'
Priscilla Presley, in *Careless Love: The Unmaking of Elvis Presley*.

Elvis with Priscilla and a new-born Lisa Marie in February 1968. Elvis called Lisa Marie 'a little miracle'.

To the world Elvis appeared as a larger-than-life character who had everything a man could want. Behind the scenes, Elvis was searching for the security and happiness that had gone from his life since his mother's death. When he wasn't partying he stayed up all night in his bedroom watching television, reading books about spirituality and eating junk food. He also spent millions of dollars on diamond jewellery or cars and houses for his friends and girlfriends. But the only time he felt any real joy was when he was on stage, performing for his fans.

This family photograph was taken in February 1971. Although they appear happy, Elvis was addicted to prescription drugs and Priscilla was worried about his over-spending.

Las Vegas Elvis

When Elvis played Las Vegas in the 1950s he had felt out of touch with the older audience. In July 1969 he was 34 and ready to take Vegas by storm. On the stage at the International Hotel, the gold curtains went up to reveal Elvis dressed in flamboyant clothes and accompanied by a full orchestra and backing singers. He performed many of his old hits but his voice was more expressive. He added new dance steps, including karate kicks and cartwheels. He laughed and joked with the audience as he told them about his life. It was pure showmanship, and it was rewarded with cheers and standing ovations.

Between 1969 and 1977 Elvis performed over 1,000 shows. Many of these were in Las Vegas, where his shows were sell-outs. As the years went by, his costumes became more elaborate. He became famous for his all-white jumpsuits, studded with rhinestones, and large bucket belts. As well as his old songs he introduced new ballads and gospel songs. Even when he became overweight and his looks began to fade, his fans always screamed for more.

'But as the years went by it got harder and harder to perform to a movie camera, and I really missed the people, I really missed contact with a live audience. And I just wanted to tell you how good it is to be back.' Elvis speaking to his audiences during one of his Las Vegas shows in 1969, in *Careless Love: The Unmaking of Elvis Presley.*

Elvis appears every bit the star in this early photograph from the Las Vegas years.

Backstage Drama

In 1970, during Elvis's comeback tour, he was thrilled to be playing live again and mixing with other 'showbiz' personalities. The satisfaction was short-lived though, and he soon became bored. Part of his frustration was his desire to play abroad but the Colonel was against a world tour. Following threats on his life, Elvis became very worried about his own safety. He spent large amounts of money on guns.

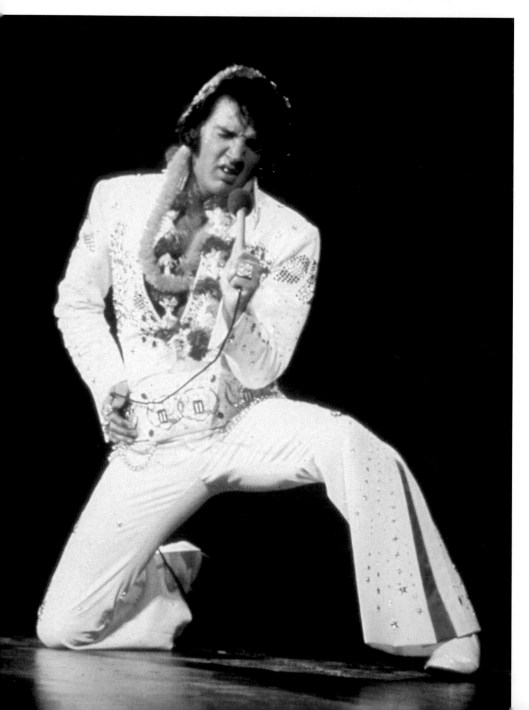

Elvis's stage act and outfits became more outrageous. His flapping flares and chunky jewellery often made him look like a ridiculous comic-book hero.

Elvis shakes hands with President Nixon in December 1970. He told the President that the Beatles were partly to blame for anti-American feeling amongst young people and hippies.

'*I talked to Vice President Agnew in Palm Springs three weeks ago and expressed my concern for our country. Sir I can and will be of any service that I can to help the country out ...*'
Taken from Elvis's letter to President Nixon, December 1970, in *Careless Love: The Unmaking of Elvis Presley.*

On 19 December 1970, Priscilla and Vernon tried to tell him that his expensive lifestyle was going to bankrupt him. Elvis flew into a rage and walked out on them. It was a mystery where he'd gone but two days later Elvis made an unannounced visit to President Nixon at the White House in Washington. The King of Rock 'n' Roll, with a face puffy from taking too many drugs, offered the President his support in the fight against illegal drugs. Elvis's offer of help was sincere but it showed how confused he was becoming.

A Fading Star

Elvis can't even raise a smile for the camera in this photograph taken in June 1972.

In December 1971 Priscilla finally left Elvis and took Lisa Marie with her. Even though he'd been unfaithful, Elvis was angry and depressed. When he released *Always on My Mind* in November 1972 it was as if he was pouring his heart into the song. By now his voice had become more soulful and he sounded hurt and full of regrets. The sadness in his own life was the price he paid for this talent.

Beautiful girlfriends and a rich lifestyle didn't fill the emptiness in Elvis's life. A high point was a charity show from Hawaii in January 1973. The show was satellite-broadcast around the world to an estimated audience of one billion. Elvis appeared slim and back on form, but within months he became bloated and ill. That year doctors pulled Elvis back from the brink of death four times after he accidentally overdosed on drugs. By 1975, Elvis was making fewer live appearances but when he did he was often dazed and forgot the words to his songs. Many people said his voice was better than ever, but for Elvis the starlight had begun to fade.

'The Living Legend was fat and ludicrously aping his former self ... His personality was lost in one of the most ill-prepared, unsteady, and most disheartening performances of his Las Vegas career.'
From a concert review in the *Hollywood Reporter* in 1973, in *Elvis Day By Day*.

Elvis tries to recapture some of his old magic back on stage performing to his adoring fans.

'Elvis Has Left the Building'

Elvis played his final show on 26 June 1977 in Indianapolis. He planned to tour again, but on 16 August he was found dead in his bathroom at Graceland with the book *The Search for the Face of Jesus* at his side. Elvis was just 42 years old but he'd died of a heart attack, brought on by years of drug abuse and over-eating. When the news broke later that day, huge crowds gathered outside Graceland to pay their final respects. All over the world shocked fans tried to come to terms with the death of the King of Rock 'n' Roll.

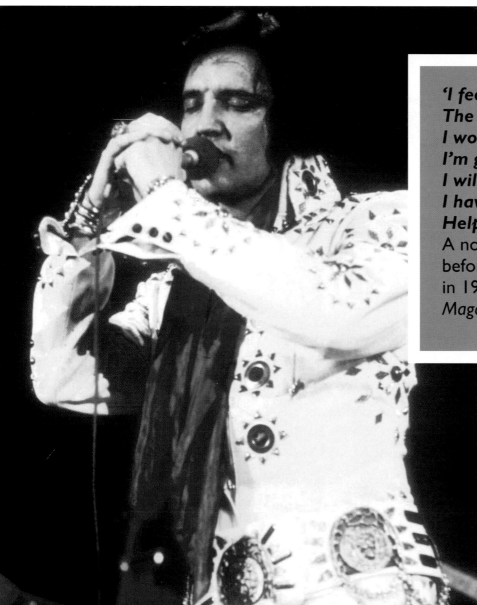

*'I feel so alone sometimes
The night is quiet for me
I would love to be able to sleep
I'm glad everyone is gone now
I will probably not rest tonight
I have no need for all of this
Help me Lord.'*
A note made by Elvis a few days before his final Las Vegas show in 1976, in *Mojo: The Music Magazine*, April 2002.

In June 1977 Elvis released **Way Down**, the last single to be released during his lifetime. Even though Elvis looked 'way down', his voice still sounded good.

The final resting place of Elvis Presley. Tours of Graceland, which began in 1982, include a few quiet moments at the graveside of the 'King'.

Today, Elvis's resting place is next to his mother and father in the Meditation Garden behind Graceland. Each August on the anniversary of his death, thousands of fans still make a pilgrimage to Graceland. Many Elvis fans claim that the King will never die. When a remixed version of the 1968 hit *A Little Less Conversation* was released in summer 2002 it seemed they were proved right. Once more the King went to the top of the charts, and a whole new generation of music-lovers was introduced to his music.

Glossary

Ballad A slow sentimental song.

Bluegrass Country and western style music usually played on the mandolin, banjos and guitars.

Blues Sad music first sung by black Americans in the early twentieth century.

Fusion Blending different styles into one.

Ghettos A poor area to live.

GI A soldier in the US Army.

Gospel music A style of black American vocals that developed from the songs sung in Baptist and Pentecostal churches in the southern states of the USA.

Gyrate To move round and round in a circle or spiral.

Hillbilly A poor person from the rural southern states of the USA.

Jamboree An organized gathering of people to celebrate a certain occasion.

National Service Compulsory work in the army of your country.

Pilgrimage A journey to a place of worship, usually a holy place.

Prescription tablets Drugs given to an individual by their doctor.

Quiff Hair that is combed upwards to form a tuft above the forehead.

Rhinestones Artificial gems sewn onto clothes to look like real jewellery.

Rhythm and blues A type of music that fuses the blues with the rhythm of jazz.

Rock 'n' roll A type of guitar and drum-based music, which blends rhythm and blues with country and western styles.

Spiritual Concerned with the spirit – such as beliefs – rather than material things.

Standing ovation Standing up and clapping with much enthusiasm.

The Great Depression A time from 1929 throughout the 1930s when there was much unemployment and economic hardship in the USA.

Further Information

Books to Read:

All Shook Up: The Life and Death of Elvis Presley by Barry Denenberg (Scholastic, 2001)

Profiles: Elvis Presley by Rupert Matthews (Heinemann, 2001)

Sources:

Down at the End of Lonely Street: The Life and Death of Elvis Presley by Peter Brown and Pat Broeske (Arrow Books, 1998)

Careless Love: The Unmaking of Elvis Presley by Peter Guralnick (Abacus, 1999)

Last Train to Memphis: The Rise of Elvis Presley by Peter Guralnick (Abacus, 1994)

Elvis Day by Day: The Definitive Record of His Life and Music by Peter Guralnick and Ernst Jorgensen (Ballantine Books, 1999)

Almost Grown: The Rise of Rock by James Miller (William Heinemann, 1999)

Date Chart

1935, 8 January Elvis Aaron Presley is born in Tupelo, Mississippi, USA.

1954, July Elvis records *That's All Right* and *Blue Moon of Kentucky* at Memphis Recording Service. Elvis plays live at Overton Park. Elvis is signed to Sun Records.

1955, August Colonel Parker becomes Elvis's manager.

21 November Elvis is signed to RCA records.

1956, 28 January Elvis appears on American television for the first time.

April *Heartbreak Hotel* reaches number one in the American charts, and also becomes his first release in the UK.

July-November Elvis releases *Don't Be Cruel, Hound Dog, Blue Suede Shoes* and *Love Me Tender*.

November Elvis's first movie *Love Me Tender* is released in the USA.

1957, March-November Elvis releases *All Shook Up* and *Jailhouse Rock*, Elvis buys Graceland in Memphis.

1958, August Gladys Presley dies of liver failure.

1959, September Elvis meets Priscilla Beaulieu.

1960, March-November Elvis releases the single *Stuck on You* and *Are You Lonesome Tonight?* Elvis's film *GI Blues* is released in the USA.

May Elvis appears on the Frank Sinatra Show and sings a duet with Sinatra.

1965, August The Beatles visit Elvis at his home in Hollywood.

1967, 1 May Elvis marries Priscilla Beaulieu in Las Vegas.

1968, 1 February Elvis's first child – Lisa Marie – is born.

November-December Elvis releases *If I Can Dream,* which he sings on a television special watched by 42 per cent of the viewing audience in the USA.

1969, April-August Elvis releases *In the Ghetto* and *Suspicious Minds.*

July Elvis opens his month-long engagement in Las Vegas at the International Hotel.

1970, 21 December Elvis meets President Nixon in the White House, Washington.

1977, June Elvis plays his final live show at Market Square Arena, Indianapolis, Indiana. Elvis's last single, *Way Down,* is released and reached number one after his death.

16, August Elvis dies at Graceland in Memphis, Tennessee.

October Following attempts to steal his body, Elvis's body is moved to the Meditation Garden behind Graceland and laid to rest next to his mother.

2002 *A Little Less Conversation,* the first re-mix of an Elvis song, reaches number one in the UK and USA as well as topping the charts in countries all over the world.

Index

All numbers in **bold** refer to pictures as well as text.